Yesterday, Today, and Tomorrow

Craig Wright

T0369566

Name _____

Age _____

Class _____

OXFORD
UNIVERSITY PRESS

OXFORD

UNIVERSITY PRESS

Great Clarendon Street, Oxford OX2 6DP

Oxford University Press is a department of the University of Oxford.
It furthers the University's objective of excellence in research, scholarship,
and education by publishing worldwide in

Oxford New York

Auckland Cape Town Dar es Salaam Hong Kong Karachi
Kuala Lumpur Madrid Melbourne Mexico City Nairobi
New Delhi Shanghai Taipei Toronto

With offices in

Argentina Austria Brazil Chile Czech Republic France Greece
Guatemala Hungary Italy Japan South Korea Poland Portugal
Singapore Switzerland Thailand Turkey Ukraine Vietnam

OXFORD and OXFORD ENGLISH are registered trade marks of
Oxford University Press in the UK and in certain other countries

ISBN-13: 978 0 19 440108 1
ISBN-10: 0 19 440108 1

Printed in China

Illustrations by: Sébastien Messerschmidt (pages 2, 4, 6, 8, 10, 12, 14, 16, 18, 20,
22, 24, 26, 28, 30) and Mark Ruffle (activities and picture dictionary, in the style
of Sébastien Messerschmidt; pages 7, 11, 15, 17, 19, 21, 23, 32, 33)

With thanks to Sally Spray for her contribution to this series

To Kuo Cheng-Shiung and Kuo Chen Yue-Shia

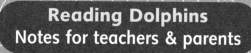
Using the book

1 Begin by looking at the first story page (page 2). Look at the picture and ask questions about it. Then read the story text under the picture with your students. **Use section 1 of the CD for this if possible.**

2 Teach and check the understanding of any new vocabulary. Note that some of the words are in the **Picture Dictionary** at the back of the book.

3 Now look at the activities on the right-hand page. Show the example to the students and instruct them to complete the activities. This may be done individually, in pairs, or as a class.

4 Do the same for the remaining pages of the book.

5 Retell the whole story more quickly, reinforcing the new vocabulary. **Section 2 of the CD can help with this.**

6 **If possible, listen to the expanded story (section 3 of the CD). The students should follow in their books.**

7 When the book is finished, use the **Picture Dictionary** to check that students understand and remember new vocabulary. **Section 4 of the CD can help with this.**

Using the CD

The CD contains four sections.

1 The story told slowly, with pauses. Use this during the first reading. It may also be used for "Listen and repeat" activities at any point.

2 The story told at normal speed. This should be used once the students have read the book for the first time.

3 The expanded story. The story is told in a longer version. This will help the students understand English when it is spoken faster, as they will now know the story and the vocabulary.

4 Vocabulary. Each word in the **Picture Dictionary** is spoken and then used in a simple sentence.

Gary and Lesley are students. They are at the museum today with their teacher and their classmates. They are walking into the Past section.

Circle the correct words and rewrite.

❶ Gary and Lesley ~~is~~ (are) students.

Gary and Lesley are students.

❷ The students are ~~at~~ / going to the museum.

❸ There ~~is~~ / are seven students in the class.

❹ There / Their teacher is a man.

❺ Gary is Lesley / Lesley's classmate.

❻ They are walking through / into the Past section.

"What clothes did people wear in the old days?" asks Gary.

"In England they wore long dresses and top hats," says the teacher. "In America they wore warm leather clothes. In China they wore beautiful silk clothes."

Answer the questions.

❶ What clothes did people wear in England?

Long dresses and top hats.

❷ Did the men wear long dresses?

_____

❸ What clothes did people wear in America?

_____

❹ Did their clothes keep them warm?

_____

❺ What clothes did people wear in China?

_____

❻ Did the boys and girls wear the same clothes?

_____

❼ What clothes did you wear yesterday?

_____

❽ Did you choose what to wear yesterday?

_____

"How did people travel?" asks Lesley.

"In America some people traveled by canoe," says the teacher. "In China they used rickshaws, and in England they traveled by horse and carriage."

1 Rearrange the words.

❶ they did how in travel China ?

How did they travel in China?

❷ by they rickshaw traveled

_____

❸ how travel in they America did ?

_____

❹ traveled by canoe they

_____

❺ did England travel how in they ?

_____

❻ horse by they carriage traveled and

_____

2 Write "in" or "on".

on a camel   _____ a rickshaw   _____ a horse

"Where did the people live in those days?"
asks Gary.

"In China people lived in big houses
with a square courtyard," says the teacher.
"In England they lived in tall, narrow
houses, and in America some people lived
in tepees."

Rewrite the sentences in the past tense.

❶ In China, people live in big houses.

In China, people lived in big houses.

❷ Kayla lives in a tepee.

_____

❸ Joseph lives in a tall, narrow house.

_____

❹ In America, children go to school on a horse.

_____

❺ Ming goes to school in a rickshaw.

_____

❻ Anne goes to school in a horse and carriage.

_____

❼ In England, people wear long dresses and top hats.

_____

"Did they have telephones in those days?"
asks Lesley.

"No, they didn't," says the teacher.
"In England they used telegrams. In China
they wrote beautiful letters, and in America
they sometimes even used smoke signals."

Look at this picture of the past.
Find the mistakes.

❶ <u>People didn't have cellphones.</u>

❷ _____

❸ _____

❹ _____

❺ _____

❻ _____

❼ _____

Now, the students are going into the
Present section of the museum.

They are having a great time. Lesley
enjoyed learning about the past. Gary
wants to see what is in the present.

1 Answer the questions.

❶ Where are the students and the teacher?

They are at the museum.

❷ Are they having a good time?

_____

❸ Did Lesley like the Past section?

_____

❹ What does Gary want to see?

_____

2 Circle the correct words.

❶ The students (were) / are in the Past section.

❷ The students were / are going into the Present section.

❸ The students are enjoyed / enjoying their visit to the museum.

13

"What clothes do we wear these days?"

"We wear jeans, sneakers, and T-shirts," says Gary.

"Girls wear skirts, blouses, and hats," says Lesley.

"We also wear caps, sandals, and jackets," says Gary.

Label and write.

1. Tom is wearing a ___cap___, a _____,

   a _____, _____, _____, and _____.

2. Jane is wearing a _____, a _____,

   a _____, a _____, _____, and

   a _____.

"How do people get around?" asks the teacher.

"I go to school by car," says Lesley.

"My dad sometimes takes me to the shops on his scooter," says Gary.

"OK. Some people also get around by motorcycle, and others use the bus."

Answer the questions.

❶ How does Jack go to school?

❷ How does May go to the park?

❸ How do Joe and Kelly go home?

❹ How does Miss Barnes go to school?

❺ How does Mr. Wood go to work?

❻ How do you go to school?

"Where do people live these days?"

"I live in an apartment, in a tall building," says Lesley.

"We live in a house with a big yard," says Gary. "My dog lives in a house, too."

Who lives in which house?
Write the correct name under each house.

Jill, Mary, Mark, Todd, and Harry live in this street.

Todd lives in a big house with two floors.

Mary and Harry live in houses with red roofs.

Harry lives in a house with two windows.

Mark lives on the fourth floor.

Jill lives in a house next to an apartment building.

Mary lives in a very small house.

"How do we communicate with other people?" asks the teacher.

"We can use a telephone or cellphone to call our friends," says Lesley.

"I use the Internet to e-mail my cousin in New Zealand," says Gary.

Read and connect in order. Write.

Martin telephones Mandy and asks her a question. Mandy doesn't know, so she e-mails Bill. Bill doesn't know, so he faxes Alan, but he doesn't know either. Alan calls Mandy on his cellphone. Mandy then e-mails Betty, and she writes a letter to Martin. Finally, Martin phones Bill to say he knows the answer.

The teacher and the children are now going into the Future section of the museum.

Nobody knows what the future will bring. But let's try to imagine.

Complete with the correct tenses.

① Past: People ate meat.

    Present: People eat meat.

    Future: People will eat meat.

② Past: Students went to school.

    Present: Students go to school.

    Future: _____

③ Past: I played with my friend.

    Present: _____

    Future: _____

④ Past: _____

    Present: She watches TV.

    Future: _____

⑤ Past: _____

    Present: _____

    Future: We will do our homework.

"What clothes will people wear in twenty years time?" asks the teacher.

"I think the clothes will be very cool," says Gary. "They will have small computers in their clothes, and the clothes will change size and color."

1 Circle these words in the box.

time	wear	cool	computer
clothes	change	twenty	will
years	think	people	size

p	e	o	p	l	e	o	c	n	s
w	i	l	l	c	o	o	l	e	i
c	d	a	y	o	o	u	o	r	z
h	c	t	i	m	e	l	t	y	e
a	o	w	t	p	h	e	h	e	s
n	w	e	i	u	l	w	e	a	r
g	l	n	s	t	p	e	s	r	a
e	k	t	e	e	n	g	l	s	i
s	h	y	☺	r	t	h	i	n	k

2 Write the secret sentence using the uncircled letters. One

25

"How will children go to school?" asks the teacher.

"I think they will go to school in cars that can fly," says Lesley.

"I think children will not go to school," says Gary. "They will have class at home on their computers."

Make sentences about the future from the squares. Use "will" or "will not".

Children	fly to school	People
have class at home	will will not	use computers
Teachers	use books and pens	Students

use telegrams	Students	speak to computers
People	will will not	Children
wear cool clothes	Teachers	wear animal skins

Children will fly to school.

27

"Where will people live in the future?"
asks Lesley.

"I think we will live in tall buildings
controlled by computers," says the
teacher.

"I think we will live in cities under the
sea," says Gary.

Change the words and write new sentences.

They live in a tepee.

She lives in a tepee.   (She)

_____ (lived)

_____ (house)

_____ (I)

_____ (an apartment)

_____ (didn't live)

_____ (He)

_____ (will)

_____ (under the sea)

_____ (have class)

_____ (at home)

_____ (We)

"How will people talk to each other in the future?" asks the teacher.

"They will use little telephones in their ears."

"They will talk to each other by just thinking and not speaking," says Lesley.

"I can't wait for the future," says Gary.

Complete the report about this book.

Book Report

Title: _____

Author: _____

Illustrator: _____

Publisher: _____

Number of pages: _____

This story is about _____

_____

New words I learned in this book

_____ _____

_____ _____

_____ _____

I think this story is...

☐ ☆☆☆☆☆ interesting

☐ ☆☆☆☆ good

☐ ☆☆☆ not bad

☐ ☆☆ OK

☐ ☆ boring

Picture Dictionary

apartment building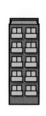

carriage

blouse

cellphone

camel

clothes

canoe

dress

horse

sandals

jacket

smoke

museum

sneakers

rickshaw

tepee

Dolphin Readers

Dolphin Readers are available at five levels, from Starter to 4.

The Dolphins series covers four major themes:

Grammar, Living Together, The World Around Us, Science and Nature.

For each theme, there are two titles at every level.

Activity Books are available for all Dolphins.

All Dolphins are available on audio CD.
(2 TITLES ON EACH CD ⟡ SEE TABLE BELOW)

Teacher's Notes are available at **www.oup.com/elt/dolphins**

	Grammar	Living Together	The World Around Us	Science and Nature
Starter	• Silly Squirrel • Monkeying Around	• My Family • A Day with Baby	• Doctor, Doctor • Moving House	• A Game of Shapes • Baby Animals
Level 1	• Meet Molly • Where Is It?	• Little Helpers • Jack the Hero	• On Safari • Lost Kitten	• Number Magic • How's the Weather?
Level 2	• Double Trouble • Super Sam	• Candy for Breakfast • Lost!	• A Visit to the City • Matt's Mistake	• Numbers, Numbers Everywhere • Circles and Squares
Level 3	• Students in Space • What Did You Do Yesterday?	• New Girl in School • Uncle Jerry's Great Idea	• Just Like Mine • Wonderful Wild Animals	• Things That Fly • Let's Go to the Rainforest
Level 4	• The Tough Task • Yesterday, Today, and Tomorrow	• We Won the Cup • Up and Down	• Where People Live • City Girl, Country Boy	• In the Ocean • Go, Gorillas, Go